Better Homes and Gardens.

Stir-Fries

Easy Everyday Recipe Library

BETTER HOMES AND GARDENS® BOOKS
Des Moines, Iowa

EASY EVERYDAY RECIPE LIBRARY
Better Homes and Gardens® Books, An imprint of Meredith® Books
Published for Creative World Enterprises LP, West Chester, Pennsylvania
www.creativeworldcooking.com

Stir-Fries
Project Editors: Spectrum Communication Services, Inc.
Project Designers: Seif Visual Communications
Copy Chief: Catherine Hamrick
Copy and Production Editor: Terri Fredrickson
Contributing Proofreaders: Kathy Eastman, Susan J. Kling
Electronic Production Coordinator: Paula Forest
Editorial and Design Assistants: Judy Bailey, Mary Lee Gavin, Karen Schirm
Test Kitchen Director: Lynn Blanchard
Production Director: Douglas M. Johnston
Production Managers: Pam Kvitne, Marjorie J. Schenkelberg

Meredith® Books
Editor in Chief: James D. Blume
Design Director: Matt Strelecki
Managing Editor: Gregory H. Kayko

Director, Sales & Marketing, Retail: Michael A. Peterson
Director, Sales & Marketing, Special Markets: Rita McMullen
Director, Sales & Marketing, Home & Garden Center Channel: Ray Wolf
Director, Operations: George A. Susral

Vice President, General Manager: Jamie L. Martin

Better Homes and Gardens® Magazine
Editor in Chief: Jean LemMon
Executive Food Editor: Nancy Byal

Meredith Publishing Group
President, Publishing Group: Christopher M. Little
Vice President, Consumer Marketing & Development: Hal Oringer

Meredith Corporation
Chairman and Chief Executive Officer: William T. Kerr

Chairman of the Executive Committee: E. T. Meredith III

Creative World Enterprises LP
Publisher: Richard J. Petrone
Design Consultants to Creative World Enterprises: Coastline Studios, Orlando, Florida

All of us at Better Homes and Gardens® Books are dedicated to providing you with the information and ideas you need to create delicious foods. We welcome your comments and suggestions. Write to us at: Better Homes and Gardens Books, Cookbook Editorial Department, 1716 Locust St., Des Moines, Iowa 50309-3023.

Our seal assures you that every recipe in *Stir-Fries* has been tested in the Better Homes and Gardens® Test Kitchen. This means that each recipe is practical and reliable, and meets our high standards of taste appeal. We guarantee your satisfaction with this book for as long as you own it.

Cover photo: Chicken, Bean, & Tomato Stir-Fry (see recipe, page 30)

Stir-frying—easy, varied, and fun. It's easy!
Even a beginner will find it a cinch to learn with our
simple-to-follow directions.

For variety, sample recipes as diverse as Cashew Pork and
Broccoli, Szechwan-Style Chicken,
Scallops in Curry Sauce, and Sesame Vegetables.

And best of all, it's fun! So pull out your wok or
skillet and start cooking! In minutes you can stir-fry
a great-tasting, healthful meal for your family.

CONTENTS

Shredded Beef and Carrots

China's Szechwan province has a distinctively hot and spicy cuisine. The spicy heat in this dish is tempered by the spicy sweetness of hoisin sauce.

12 ounces beef top round steak
2 tablespoons dry sherry
2 tablespoons soy sauce
1 tablespoon hoisin sauce
1 tablespoon hot bean sauce or
    hot bean paste
2 teaspoons sugar
2 teaspoons grated gingerroot
1 teaspoon toasted sesame oil
1 clove garlic, minced
½ teaspoon crushed red pepper
¼ teaspoon black pepper
1 tablespoon cooking oil
3 medium carrots, cut into julienne
    strips (1½ cups)
2 cups hot cooked rice
2 green onions, thinly bias-sliced

Trim fat from meat. Partially freeze meat. Thinly slice across the grain into bite-size strips. Cut strips in half lengthwise. Set aside.

For sauce, in a small bowl stir together the sherry, soy sauce, hoisin sauce, bean sauce or paste, sugar, gingerroot, sesame oil, garlic, crushed red pepper, and black pepper. Set aside.

Add cooking oil to a wok or large skillet. Preheat over medium-high heat (add more oil if necessary during cooking). Stir-fry carrots in hot oil for 3 to 4 minutes or till crisp-tender. Remove carrots from wok.

Add meat to wok. Stir-fry for 2 to 3 minutes or to desired doneness. Push meat from center of wok.

Add sauce to center of wok. Cook and stir till bubbly. Return cooked carrots to wok. Stir all ingredients together to coat. Cook and stir about 2 minutes more or till heated through.

Serve immediately with hot rice. Sprinkle rice with green onions. Makes 4 servings.

Nutrition information per serving: 314 calories, 24 g protein, 31 g carbohydrate, 9 g fat (2 g saturated fat), 54 mg cholesterol, 1,086 mg sodium.

Thai Beef Larnar

In Thai cuisine, fish sauce is a common ingredient used to salt foods. In this recipe it seasons the Nam Prik—Thailand's version of bottled hot pepper sauce.

Nam Prik
1 pound beef top round steak
1 tablespoon cooking oil
4 cups broccoli flowerets
2 cups hot cooked rice
  Chili pepper flower (optional)

Prepare Nam Prik. Set aside. Trim fat from meat. Partially freeze meat. Thinly slice across the grain into bite-size strips. Set aside.

Add cooking oil to a wok or large skillet. Preheat over medium-high heat (add more oil if necessary during cooking). Stir-fry broccoli in hot oil for 3 to 4 minutes or till crisp-tender. Remove broccoli from wok.

Add half of the meat to wok. Stir-fry for 2 to 3 minutes or to desired doneness. Remove from wok. Repeat with the remaining meat. Return all of the meat to the wok. Return broccoli to wok.

Add Nam Prik. Stir all ingredients together to coat. Bring to boiling. Cover and cook about 1 minute more or till heated through. Serve immediately with hot cooked rice. If desired, garnish with chili flower. Makes 4 servings.

Nam Prik: Remove stems and seeds from 2 to 4 *dried red chili peppers.* Place peppers in a small bowl and cover with *boiling water.* Let stand for 45 minutes. Drain. Chop peppers. (Or, substitute ½ to 1 teaspoon *crushed red pepper* and continue as directed.) In a blender container combine chili peppers or crushed red pepper; ¼ cup *water;* 2 tablespoons *lemon juice;* 2 tablespoons *soy sauce;* 1 tablespoon *cooking oil;* 2 to 4 cloves *garlic,* quartered; and 1 to 1½ teaspoons *fish sauce* or *nuoc cham.* Cover and blend till mixture is nearly smooth.

Nutrition information per serving: 363 calories, 33 g protein, 30 g carbohydrate, 13 g fat (3 g saturated fat), 73 mg cholesterol, 662 mg sodium.

Sweet-and-Sour Steak

The sweet-and-sour dishes of Canton are among the most familiar types of Chinese food. They are said to have evolved in response to the demanding tastes of the foreigners in this large port city.

8 ounces beef top round steak
1 small orange
1 15¼-ounce can pineapple chunks
    (juice pack)
2 tablespoons vinegar
2 tablespoons soy sauce
1 tablespoon cornstarch
1 tablespoon brown sugar
⅛ teaspoon ground red pepper
1 tablespoon cooking oil
1 medium green sweet pepper, cut
    into 1-inch pieces
1 small onion, cut into thin wedges
2 cups hot cooked rice
    Orange slices (optional)

Trim fat from meat. Partially freeze meat. Thinly slice across the grain into bite-size strips. Set aside. Peel and section orange. Set aside.

For sauce, drain pineapple, reserving juice. Pour ½ cup of the reserved juice into a small bowl. (Reserve remaining juice for another use.) Stir in the vinegar, soy sauce, cornstarch, brown sugar, and ground red pepper. Set aside.

Add cooking oil to a wok or large skillet. Preheat over medium-high heat (add more oil if necessary during cooking). Stir-fry green pepper and onion in hot oil for 3 to 4 minutes or till crisp-tender. Remove the vegetables from wok.

Add meat to wok. Stir-fry for 2 to 3 minutes or to desired doneness. Push meat from center of wok. Stir sauce; add to center of wok. Cook and stir till thickened and bubbly.

Return cooked vegetables to wok. Add pineapple chunks. Stir all ingredients together to coat. Cook and stir about 2 minutes more or till heated through. Stir in orange sections. Serve immediately over hot rice. If desired, garnish with orange slices. Makes 4 servings.

Nutrition information per serving: 326 calories, 17 g protein, 51 g carbohydrate, 7 g fat (2 g saturated fat), 36 mg cholesterol, 545 mg sodium.

Oriental Beef and Noodles

Want more Oriental flavor? Substitute ¼ teaspoon of five-spice powder for the ground ginger.

1	3-ounce package Oriental noodles with beef flavor
8	ounces boneless beef sirloin steak, cut ¾ inch thick
1	tablespoon cooking oil
1	medium carrot, thinly sliced
1	stalk celery, bias-sliced
1	6-ounce package frozen pea pods, thawed
¼	cup water
1	tablespoon snipped parsley
2	teaspoons teriyaki sauce
½	teaspoon ground ginger
¼	teaspoon crushed red pepper (optional)

Cook the Oriental noodles according to package directions, except drain the noodles and reserve the seasoning package.

Meanwhile, trim fat from meat. Partially freeze meat. Thinly slice into bite-size strips. Set aside.

Add cooking oil to a wok or large skillet. Preheat over medium-high heat (add more oil if necessary during cooking). Stir-fry carrot and celery in hot oil for 2 to 3 minutes or till vegetables are crisp-tender. Remove vegetables from wok.

Add the meat to wok. Stir-fry for 2 to 3 minutes or to desired doneness. Return cooked vegetables to wok.

Stir in the noodles, the reserved seasoning package, pea pods, water, parsley, teriyaki sauce, ginger, and, if desired, crushed red pepper. Cook over medium heat till heated through, stirring occasionally. Serve immediately. Makes 4 servings.

Nutrition information per serving: 621 calories, 30 g protein, 61 g carbohydrate, 30 g fat (3 g saturated fat), 50 mg cholesterol, 1,724 mg sodium.

Bias-Slicing

To bias-slice vegetables, such as celery or green onions, or meats, hold a sharp knife at a 45-degree angle to the vegetable or meat and cut into thin diagonal slices. Partially freezing meat before bias-slicing makes it easier to cut thin slices.

Southwestern Stir-Fry

Just because it comes out of a wok doesn't mean it has to taste Chinese! The proof is in the eating, so why not sample this Mexican-style stir-fry?

1   cup salsa
2   teaspoons cornstarch
8   8-inch flour tortillas
1   tablespoon cooking oil
1   medium green sweet pepper, cut
       into strips
1   11-ounce can whole kernel corn,
       drained
3   green onions, bias-sliced into
       1-inch pieces (½ cup)
1   pound lean ground beef
10 cherry tomatoes, halved
½   cup shredded cheddar cheese or
       Monterey Jack cheese with
       jalapeño peppers (2 ounces)
    Cilantro sprigs (optional)

For sauce, in a small bowl stir together the salsa and cornstarch. Set aside.

Wrap tortillas in foil and bake in a 350° oven about 10 minutes or till warm. [Or, just before serving, microwave tortillas, covered, on 100% power (high) about 1 minute or till warm.]

Meanwhile, add cooking oil to a wok or large skillet. Preheat over medium-high heat (add more oil if necessary during cooking). Stir-fry sweet pepper, corn, and green onions in hot oil about 2 minutes or till sweet pepper is crisp-tender. Remove from wok.

Crumble beef into wok. Stir-fry for 2 to 3 minutes or till brown, stirring only as necessary. Drain fat. Push meat from center of wok.

Stir sauce; add to center of wok. Cook and stir till thickened and bubbly. Return the cooked vegetables to wok. Stir all ingredients together to coat. Stir in the tomatoes; reduce heat. Cover and cook about 1 minute more or till heated through.

Serve immediately with tortillas. Sprinkle with cheese. If desired, garnish with cilantro. Makes 4 servings.

Nutrition information per serving: 634 calories, 31 g protein, 64 g carbohydrate, 29 g fat (10 g saturated fat), 85 mg cholesterol, 1,042 mg sodium.

Cashew Pork and Broccoli

The Portuguese brought the cashew from the New World to India and East Africa in the fifteenth century. From there it traveled to China and worked its way into Chinese cuisine.

12 ounces lean boneless pork
2 tablespoons soy sauce
2 teaspoons toasted sesame oil
2 teaspoons grated gingerroot
2 cloves garlic, minced
½ cup hoisin sauce
½ cup water
2 tablespoons soy sauce
1 tablespoon cornstarch
1 teaspoon sugar
⅛ teaspoon crushed red pepper
1 tablespoon cooking oil
2 medium onions, cut into thin wedges
2 stalks celery, thinly bias-sliced
3 cups broccoli flowerets
2 cups hot cooked rice
½ cup dry roasted cashews

Trim fat from meat. Partially freeze meat. Thinly slice across the grain into bite-size strips. In a medium bowl combine meat, 2 tablespoons soy sauce, sesame oil, gingerroot, and garlic. Cover; chill for 1 to 2 hours.

For sauce, in a small bowl stir together hoisin sauce, water, 2 tablespoons soy sauce, cornstarch, sugar, and crushed red pepper. Set aside.

Add cooking oil to a wok or large skillet. Preheat over medium-high heat (add more oil if necessary during cooking.) Stir-fry onions and celery in hot oil for 1 minute. Add broccoli; stir-fry for 3 to 4 minutes or till crisp-tender. Remove vegetables from wok.

Add meat mixture to wok. Stir-fry for 2 to 3 minutes or till meat is slightly pink in center. Push meat from center of wok.

Stir sauce; add to center of wok. Cook and stir till thickened and bubbly. Return cooked vegetables to wok. Stir all ingredients together to coat. Cover and cook about 1 minute more or till heated through. Serve immediately with hot cooked rice. Sprinkle with cashews. Makes 4 servings.

Nutrition information per serving: 480 calories, 21 g protein, 42 g carbohydrate, 26 g fat (5 g saturated fat), 38 mg cholesterol, 1,554 mg sodium.

Stir-Fried Pork and Jicama

Though jicama (HE-kuh-muh) is a Mexican vegetable, it adds some crispness to this Chinese-inspired dish.

1   pound lean boneless pork
½   cup cold water
¼   cup dry sherry
¼   cup soy sauce
4   teaspoons cornstarch
1   tablespoon cooking oil
1   teaspoon grated gingerroot
1   clove garlic, minced
½   of a medium jicama, peeled and
        cut into julienne strips (1 cup)
1   medium red or green sweet pepper,
        cut into thin strips
1   green onion, sliced
2   cups shredded spinach or Chinese
        cabbage
2   cups hot cooked rice

Trim fat from meat. Partially freeze meat. Thinly slice across the grain into bite-size strips. Set aside.

For sauce, in a small bowl stir together water, sherry, soy sauce, and cornstarch. Set aside.

Add cooking oil to a wok or large skillet. Preheat over medium-high heat (add more oil if necessary during cooking). Stir-fry gingerroot and garlic in hot oil for 15 seconds. Add jicama, sweet pepper, and green onion. Stir-fry for 1 to 2 minutes or till crisp-tender. Remove vegetables from wok.

Add half of the meat to wok. Stir-fry for 2 to 3 minutes or till slightly pink in center. Remove from wok. Repeat with the remaining meat. Return all of the meat to the wok. Push meat from center of wok.

Stir sauce; add to center of wok. Cook and stir till thickened and bubbly. Return cooked vegetables to wok. Stir all ingredients together to coat. Add spinach or cabbage. Cook and stir for 1 to 2 minutes more or till heated through. Serve immediately with hot cooked rice. Makes 4 servings.

Nutrition information per serving: 341 calories, 21 g protein, 35 g carbohydrate, 11 g fat (3 g saturated fat), 51 mg cholesterol, 1,080 mg sodium.

Pork and Pear Stir-Fry

Plum preserves, pears, and gingerroot give this delicious pork entrée its special sweetness.

1 pound pork tenderloin
½ cup plum preserves
3 tablespoons soy sauce
2 tablespoons lemon juice
1 tablespoon prepared horseradish
2 teaspoons cornstarch
½ teaspoon crushed red pepper
1 tablespoon cooking oil
2 teaspoons grated gingerroot
1 medium yellow or green sweet
  pepper, cut into julienne strips
1 medium pear, cored and sliced
⅓ cup sliced water chestnuts
1½ cups fresh pea pods, strings
  removed, or 4 ounces frozen
  pea pods, thawed
2 cups hot cooked rice

Trim fat from meat. Partially freeze meat. Thinly slice across the grain into bite-size strips. Set aside.

For sauce, in a small bowl stir together plum preserves, soy sauce, lemon juice, horseradish, cornstarch, and crushed red pepper. Set aside.

Add cooking oil to a wok or large skillet. Preheat over medium-high heat (add more oil if necessary during cooking). Stir-fry gingerroot in hot oil for 15 seconds. Add sweet pepper and pear; stir-fry for 1½ minutes. Remove pear mixture from wok.

Add half of the meat to wok. Stir-fry for 2 to 3 minutes or till slightly pink in center. Remove from wok. Repeat with the remaining meat. Return all of the meat to the wok. Push meat from center of wok.

Stir sauce; add to center of wok. Cook and stir till slightly thickened and bubbly.

Return pear mixture to wok. Add water chestnuts. Stir all ingredients together to coat. Cook and stir for 2 minutes. Add pea pods. Cover and cook for 1 to 2 minutes more or till heated through. Serve immediately with hot cooked rice. Makes 4 servings.

Nutrition information per serving: 473 calories, 30 g protein, 70 g carbohydrate, 8 g fat (2 g saturated fat), 81 mg cholesterol, 884 mg sodium.

Polynesian Stir-Fry

This tangy sweet dish featuring a colorful mix of pineapple chunks and vegetables can be made with your choice of pork, lamb, or beef.

12 ounces lean boneless pork, lamb, or beef
3 tablespoons cider vinegar
3 tablespoons soy sauce
1 tablespoon brown sugar
1 teaspoon dry mustard
1 teaspoon grated gingerroot
¼ teaspoon black pepper
1 8-ounce can pineapple chunks (juice pack)
2 teaspoons cornstarch
1 tablespoon cooking oil
1 medium onion, chopped
2 small zucchini, cut into julienne strips (1½ cups)
1 medium red or green sweet pepper, cut into 1-inch squares
2 cups hot cooked rice

Trim fat from meat. Partially freeze meat. Thinly slice across the grain into bite-size strips.

In a medium bowl stir together the meat, vinegar, soy sauce, brown sugar, dry mustard, gingerroot, and black pepper. Let stand for 15 minutes. Drain meat, reserving soy mixture. Set aside.

Drain pineapple, reserving juice. For sauce, in a small bowl stir together the reserved pineapple juice, soy mixture, and cornstarch. Set aside.

Add cooking oil to a wok or large skillet. Preheat over medium-high heat (add more oil if necessary during cooking). Stir-fry onion in hot oil for 2 minutes. Add zucchini and sweet pepper. Stir-fry about 1½ minutes more or till vegetables are crisp-tender. Remove the vegetables from wok.

Add meat to wok. Stir-fry for 2 to 3 minutes or till slightly pink in center. Push meat from center of wok.

Stir sauce; add to center of wok. Cook and stir till thickened and bubbly. Return cooked vegetables to wok. Add pineapple. Stir all ingredients together to coat. Cook and stir for 1 to 2 minutes more or till heated through. Serve immediately over hot cooked rice. Makes 4 servings.

Nutrition information per serving: 317 calories, 16 g protein, 42 g carbohydrate, 10 g fat (2 g saturated fat), 38 mg cholesterol, 806 mg sodium.

Jamaican Pork & Sweet Potato Stir-Fry

Take a vacation from the postwork, predinner rush with this Jamaica-inspired dish that features two of this easygoing island's favorite ingredients: lean pork and golden sweet potatoes. For flavor, pick up Jamaican jerk seasoning in the grocery store spice aisle or make your own seasoning.

1½ cups quick-cooking rice
2   green onions, thinly sliced (¼ cup)
1   large sweet potato (about 12 ounces)
1   medium tart apple (such as Granny Smith), cored
12 ounces lean boneless pork strips for stir-frying
2   to 3 teaspoons purchased or homemade Jamaican jerk seasoning
1   tablespoon cooking oil
⅓ cup apple juice or water

Prepare rice according to package directions. Stir half of the green onions into cooked rice.

Meanwhile, peel sweet potato. Cut into quarters lengthwise, then thinly slice crosswise. Place in a microwave-safe pie plate or shallow dish. Cover with vented plastic wrap. Microwave on 100% power (high) for 3 to 4 minutes or till tender, stirring once. Cut apple into 16 wedges. Sprinkle meat strips with Jamaican jerk seasoning; toss to coat evenly.

Add cooking oil to a wok or large skillet. Preheat over medium-high heat (add more oil if necessary during cooking). Stir-fry meat in hot oil for 2 minutes. Add apple and the remaining green onions. Stir-fry for 1 to 2 minutes or till meat is slightly pink in center.

Stir in sweet potato and apple juice or water. Bring to boiling; reduce heat. Simmer, uncovered, for 1 minute more. Serve immediately over hot rice mixture. Makes 4 servings.

Homemade Jamaican Jerk Seasoning: In a small mixing bowl combine 1 teaspoon *crushed red pepper;* ½ teaspoon ground *allspice;* ¼ teaspoon *curry powder;* ¼ teaspoon *coarsely ground black pepper;* ⅛ teaspoon dried *thyme,* crushed; ⅛ teaspoon *ground red pepper;* and ⅛ teaspoon ground *ginger.*

Nutrition information per serving: 365 calories, 16 g protein, 54 g carbohydrate, 9 g fat (2 g saturated fat), 38 mg cholesterol, 131 mg sodium.

Pork with Apricots and Peppers

The zesty flavors of golden apricots, Dijon-style mustard, and fresh garlic lend themselves well to this non-Oriental pork stir-fry.

12	ounces lean boneless pork
½	cup dry white wine or chicken broth
⅓	cup dried apricots, cut into thin strips, or ⅓ cup mixed dried fruit bits
¼	cup water
2	teaspoons cornstarch
2	teaspoons sugar
1	teaspoon Dijon-style mustard
½	teaspoon dried oregano, crushed
¼	teaspoon salt
¼	teaspoon black pepper
1	tablespoon cooking oil
2	cloves garlic, minced
1	medium onion, cut into thin wedges
1	large green sweet pepper, cut into 1-inch squares
2	cups hot cooked rice

Trim fat from meat. Partially freeze meat. Thinly slice across the grain into bite-size strips. Set aside.

For sauce, in a medium bowl combine wine or broth, apricots or dried fruit bits, water, cornstarch, sugar, mustard, oregano, salt, and black pepper. Set aside.

Add cooking oil to a wok or large skillet. Preheat over medium-high heat (add more oil if necessary during cooking). Stir-fry garlic in hot oil for 15 seconds. Add onion; stir-fry for 1½ minutes. Add sweet pepper; stir-fry about 1½ minutes more or till crisp-tender. Remove vegetables from wok.

Add meat to wok. Stir-fry for 2 to 3 minutes or till slightly pink in center. Push meat from center of wok.

Stir sauce; add to center of wok. Cook and stir till thickened and bubbly. Return cooked vegetables to wok. Stir all ingredients together to coat. Cook and stir for 1 to 2 minutes more or till heated through. Serve immediately with hot rice. Makes 4 servings.

Nutrition information per serving: 331 calories, 16 g protein, 41 g carbohydrate, 10 g fat (3 g saturated fat), 38 mg cholesterol, 201 mg sodium.

Greek Lamb Stir-Fry

Oregano and rosemary join with lemon juice, olive oil, and feta cheese to lend this delicious lamb dish some of the characteristic flavors of Greece.

8	ounces lean boneless lamb
1	tablespoon olive oil or cooking oil
1	tablespoon lemon juice or balsamic vinegar
½	teaspoon dried rosemary, crushed
½	teaspoon dried oregano, crushed
¼	teaspoon pepper
1	tablespoon cooking oil
1	clove garlic, minced
1	medium carrot, thinly bias-sliced
1	small red onion, thinly sliced (⅓ cup)
4	cups torn spinach (about 5 ounces)
2	small tomatoes, cut into thin wedges
2	cups hot cooked rice (optional)
¼	cup crumbled feta cheese (1 ounce)

Trim fat from meat. Partially freeze meat. Thinly slice across the grain into bite-size strips. Set aside. For sauce, in a small bowl combine 1 tablespoon olive or cooking oil, lemon juice or vinegar, rosemary, oregano, and pepper. Set aside.

Add 1 tablespoon cooking oil to a wok or large skillet. Preheat over medium-high heat (add more oil if necessary during cooking). Stir-fry garlic in hot oil for 15 seconds. Add carrot and onion; stir-fry for 3 to 4 minutes or till crisp-tender. Remove from wok.

Add meat to wok. Stir-fry for 2 to 3 minutes or to desired doneness. Return cooked vegetables to wok. Add spinach, tomato wedges, and sauce. Stir all ingredients together to coat. Remove from heat. Serve immediately. If desired, serve over hot cooked rice. Sprinkle with feta cheese. Makes 3 servings.

Nutrition information per serving: 243 calories, 16 g protein, 11 g carbohydrate, 16 g fat (4 g saturated fat), 45 mg cholesterol, 208 mg sodium.

Curried Chicken Siam

Unsweetened coconut milk, a common ingredient in Thai cuisine, is available in large supermarkets and Asian food stores. If you are unable to find it, use 1¼ cups milk mixed with ½ teaspoon coconut extract.

---

1 to 3 dried red Anaheim or California chili peppers
2 tablespoons snipped cilantro
1 teaspoon ground ginger
1 teaspoon finely shredded lime peel
1 stalk lemongrass, cut into 2-inch pieces, or 1 teaspoon finely shredded lemon peel
½ teaspoon salt
½ teaspoon ground nutmeg
½ teaspoon ground cumin
½ teaspoon ground coriander
12 ounces skinless, boneless chicken thighs
1 tablespoon cooking oil
4 cloves garlic, minced
2 medium onions, chopped
1¼ cups canned unsweetened coconut milk
1 8-ounce can sliced bamboo shoots, drained
1 medium red or green sweet pepper, cut into julienne strips
2 tablespoons snipped fresh basil or ¾ teaspoon dried basil, crushed
1 medium cucumber, halved lengthwise and sliced (optional)
Sliced leek (optional)
2 cups hot cooked rice

Remove stems and seeds from chili peppers. Place the peppers in a medium bowl and cover with boiling water. Let stand about 15 minutes or till softened. Drain. Chop chili peppers. Set aside.

Meanwhile, for spice mixture, in a small bowl combine cilantro, ginger, lime peel, lemongrass or lemon peel, salt, nutmeg, cumin, and coriander. Set aside. Rinse chicken; pat dry with paper towels. Cut into 1-inch pieces. Set aside.

Add cooking oil to a wok or large skillet. Preheat over medium-high heat (add more oil if necessary during cooking). Stir-fry garlic in hot oil for 15 seconds. Add onions; stir-fry about 2 minutes or till crisp-tender. Add spice mixture; stir-fry for 2 minutes.

Add chicken to wok. Stir-fry for 3 to 4 minutes or till tender and no longer pink. If used, discard the lemongrass. Add coconut milk, bamboo shoots, sweet pepper, and chili peppers to wok. Cook and stir for 2 to 3 minutes or till heated through. Stir in basil.

If desired, arrange cucumber slices around the rim of a serving plate. Add meat mixture to plate and, if desired, garnish with leek. Serve immediately with hot cooked rice. Makes 4 servings.

Nutrition information per serving: 466 calories, 18 g protein, 34 g carbohydrate, 29 g fat (17 g saturated fat), 41 mg cholesterol, 339 mg sodium.

Chicken Picadillo

Ask everyone to fill and roll their own tortillas right at the supper table—it makes less work for the cook and more fun for the family.

⅓   cup slivered almonds
½   cup picante sauce
2   teaspoons cornstarch
2   medium tomatoes, chopped (2 cups)
⅓   cup sliced pimiento-stuffed green
       olives
⅓   cup raisins
2   tablespoons snipped parsley
¾   teaspoon salt
¼   teaspoon black pepper
¼   teaspoon ground cinnamon
⅛   teaspoon ground cloves
1½ pounds skinless, boneless chicken
       breast halves
12 8-inch flour tortillas
1   tablespoon cooking oil
3   cloves garlic, minced
2   medium onions, chopped (1 cup)
1   medium apple, cored and chopped
2   fresh, pickled, or canned jalapeño
       peppers, seeded and chopped
       (3 tablespoons)
12 leaf lettuce leaves

Preheat a wok or 12-inch skillet over medium-high heat. Add almonds; stir-fry for 2 to 3 minutes or till golden. Remove almonds from wok. Let wok cool.

For sauce, stir together picante sauce and cornstarch. In a medium bowl stir together undrained tomatoes, olives, raisins, parsley, salt, black pepper, cinnamon, cloves, and almonds. Rinse chicken; pat dry with paper towels. Cut into thin bite-size strips. Set aside.

Wrap tortillas in foil and bake in a 350° oven about 10 minutes or till warm. [Or, just before serving, microwave tortillas, covered, on 100% power (high) about 1 minute or till warm.]

Meanwhile, add cooking oil to wok. Preheat over medium-high heat (add more oil if necessary during cooking). Stir-fry garlic in hot oil for 15 seconds. Add onions, apple, and jalapeño peppers. Stir-fry for 2 to 3 minutes or till crisp-tender. Remove from wok.

Add half of the chicken to wok. Stir-fry for 2 to 3 minutes or till tender and no longer pink. Remove from wok. Repeat with the remaining chicken. Return all of the chicken to wok. Push from center of wok.

Stir sauce; add sauce and tomato mixture to center of wok. Cook and stir till thickened and bubbly. Return apple mixture to wok. Stir all ingredients together to coat. Cook and stir for 2 minutes more. Place a lettuce leaf on each tortilla. Top with chicken mixture and roll up. Serve immediately. Makes 6 servings.

Nutrition information per serving: 500 calories, 31 g protein, 61 g carbohydrate, 16 g fat (2 g saturated fat), 59 mg cholesterol, 974 mg sodium.

Fragrant Spiced Chicken

Given Malaysia's location in the island crossroads of Southeast Asia and its importance in the spice trade, it's no surprise that the cuisine embraces a mix of cultures and uses a wealth of spices. This Malaysian dish shows a blend of both Indian and Asian influences.

12 ounces skinless, boneless chicken
      thighs
2 teaspoons ground coriander
1½ teaspoons ground cumin
1 teaspoon ground turmeric
1 teaspoon ground nutmeg
¾ teaspoon ground cinnamon
¼ teaspoon ground red pepper
¼ teaspoon ground cloves
⅔ cup water
¼ cup cider vinegar
3 tablespoons sugar
1 tablespoon cornstarch
½ teaspoon salt
1 tablespoon cooking oil
1 tablespoon grated gingerroot
4 cloves garlic, minced
2 medium onions, cut into thin
      wedges
1 medium red or green sweet pepper,
      cut into strips
½ of a stalk lemongrass, cut into
      2-inch pieces, or ½ teaspoon
      finely shredded lemon peel
2 cups hot cooked couscous or rice
3 tablespoons coarsely chopped
      roasted peanuts

Rinse chicken; pat dry with paper towels. Cut into 1-inch pieces. In a medium bowl combine coriander, cumin, turmeric, nutmeg, cinnamon, ground red pepper, and cloves. Add chicken; stir to coat. Set aside.

For sauce, in a small bowl stir together water, vinegar, sugar, cornstarch, and salt. Set aside.

Add cooking oil to a wok or large skillet. Preheat over medium-high heat (add more oil if necessary during cooking). Stir-fry gingerroot and garlic in hot oil for 15 seconds. Add onions, sweet pepper, and lemongrass or lemon peel. Stir-fry for 2 to 3 minutes or till vegetables are crisp-tender. Remove vegetables from wok. If used, discard lemongrass.

Add chicken mixture to wok. Stir-fry for 3 to 4 minutes or till chicken is tender and no longer pink, scraping bottom of wok constantly to prevent spices from sticking. Push chicken from center of wok.

Stir sauce; add to center of wok. Cook and stir till thickened and bubbly. Return cooked vegetables to wok. Stir all ingredients together to coat. Cook and stir for 1 to 2 minutes more or till heated through. Serve immediately with hot cooked couscous or rice. Sprinkle with peanuts. Makes 4 servings.

Nutrition information per serving: 350 calories, 19 g protein, 44 g carbohydrate, 12 g fat (2 g saturated fat), 41 mg cholesterol, 456 mg sodium.

Kung Pao Chicken

Kung Pao means "guardian of the throne." Legend has it that this dish was named for a general—one of the throne's guardians—who woke up hungry one night and commanded a snack. The chef had only leftover chicken and peanuts. Afraid to put leftovers before his master, the chef added lots of seasonings to mask the chicken's staleness and threw in the peanuts for good measure. The general loved it!

12 ounces skinless, boneless chicken
     breast halves
 1 tablespoon dry sherry
 1 teaspoon cornstarch
¼ cup water
¼ cup soy sauce
 4 teaspoons cornstarch
 1 tablespoon sugar
 1 teaspoon vinegar
    Few dashes bottled hot pepper sauce
 1 tablespoon cooking oil
 2 teaspoons grated gingerroot
 2 cloves garlic, minced
 6 green onions, cut into ½-inch pieces
    (1 cup)
½ cup dry roasted peanuts
 2 cups hot cooked rice
    Green onion fans (optional)

Rinse chicken; pat dry with paper towels. Cut into ¾-inch pieces. In a medium bowl stir together chicken, sherry, and 1 teaspoon cornstarch. Let stand for 15 minutes.

For sauce, in a small bowl stir together water, soy sauce, 4 teaspoons cornstarch, sugar, vinegar, and hot pepper sauce. Set aside.

Add cooking oil to a wok or large skillet. Preheat over medium-high heat (add more oil if necessary during cooking). Stir-fry gingerroot and garlic in hot oil for 15 seconds. Add chicken mixture. Stir-fry for 3 to 4 minutes or till tender and no longer pink. Push chicken from center of wok.

Stir sauce; add to center of wok. Cook and stir till thickened and bubbly. Add green onion pieces and peanuts. Stir all ingredients together to coat. Cook and stir for 1 to 2 minutes more or till heated through.

Serve immediately with hot cooked rice. If desired, garnish with green onion fans. Makes 4 servings.

Nutrition information per serving: 374 calories, 24 g protein, 35 g carbohydrate, 15 g fat (2 g saturated fat), 45 mg cholesterol, 1,220 mg sodium.

Chicken and Apple Stir-Fry

This sweet-spiced dish includes an array of colorful peppers, plus dried mushrooms, crunchy almonds, and crisp, tart apple slices.

6	dried mushrooms (such as shiitake or wood ear mushrooms)
12	ounces skinless, boneless chicken breast halves or turkey breast tenderloin steaks
¾	cup cold water
3	tablespoons frozen orange, apple, or pineapple juice concentrate, thawed
2	tablespoons soy sauce
2	teaspoons cornstarch
¼	teaspoon ground ginger
¼	teaspoon ground cinnamon
⅛	to ¼ teaspoon ground red pepper
¼	cup sliced or slivered almonds
1	tablespoon cooking oil
2	medium green, red, orange, and/or yellow sweet peppers, cut into thin strips
2	medium apples, thinly sliced
2	cups hot cooked brown rice

In a small bowl cover mushrooms with warm water. Let soak for 30 minutes. Rinse and squeeze the mushrooms to drain thoroughly. Discard stems. Thinly slice mushrooms. Set aside.

Meanwhile, rinse chicken or turkey; pat dry with paper towels. Cut into 1-inch pieces. Set aside.

For sauce, in a small bowl stir together the cold water, juice concentrate, soy sauce, cornstarch, ginger, cinnamon, and red pepper. Set aside.

Preheat a wok or large skillet over medium-high heat. Add almonds; stir-fry for 2 to 3 minutes or till golden. Remove almonds from wok. Let wok cool.

Add cooking oil to wok. Preheat over medium-high heat (add more oil if necessary during cooking). Stir-fry mushrooms, sweet peppers, and apples in hot oil for 1 to 2 minutes or till peppers and apples are crisp-tender. Remove apple mixture from wok.

Add chicken to wok. Stir-fry for 3 to 4 minutes or till tender and no longer pink. Push chicken from center of wok. Stir sauce; add to center of wok. Cook and stir till thickened and bubbly. Return apple mixture to wok. Stir all ingredients together to coat. Cook and stir for 1 to 2 minutes more or till heated through.

Stir in toasted almonds. Serve immediately over hot cooked brown rice. Makes 4 servings.

Nutrition information per serving: 370 calories, 22 g protein, 48 g carbohydrate, 11 g fat (2 g saturated fat), 45 mg cholesterol, 563 mg sodium.

Szechwan-Style Chicken

Skip the Chinese take-out and create your own delicious Oriental meal in just minutes at home.

1 pound skinless, boneless chicken
    breast halves
⅓ cup teriyaki sauce
3 tablespoons Szechwan spicy
    stir-fry sauce
2 teaspoons cornstarch
1 tablespoon cooking oil
1 large onion, chopped (1 cup)
3 cups chopped bok choy
1 cup broccoli flowerets
1 medium red sweet pepper, cut into
    thin strips
2 cups fresh pea pods, strings
    removed, or one 6-ounce package
    frozen pea pods, thawed
1 14-ounce can whole baby sweet
    corn, drained and halved
    crosswise
½ of a 15-ounce jar whole straw
    mushrooms, drained
3 cups hot cooked rice noodles or rice

Rinse chicken; pat dry with paper towels. Cut into thin bite-size strips. Set aside.

For sauce, in a small bowl stir together teriyaki sauce, stir-fry sauce, and cornstarch. Set aside.

Add cooking oil to a wok or large skillet. Preheat over medium-high heat (add more oil if necessary during cooking). Stir-fry onion in hot oil for 2 minutes. Add bok choy, broccoli, and sweet pepper. Stir-fry for 1 minute. If using, add fresh pea pods. Stir-fry for 1 to 2 minutes more or till vegetables are crisp-tender. Remove vegetables from wok.

Add half of the chicken to wok. Stir-fry for 2 to 3 minutes or till tender and no longer pink. Remove from wok. Repeat with the remaining chicken. Return all of the chicken to wok. Push from center of wok.

Stir sauce; add to center of wok. Cook and stir till thickened and bubbly. Return cooked vegetables to wok. Add corn, mushrooms, and, if using, thawed frozen pea pods. Stir all ingredients together to coat. Cook and stir about 1 minute more or till heated through. Serve immediately over hot cooked rice noodles or rice. Makes 6 servings.

Nutrition information per serving: 260 calories, 22 g protein, 32 g carbohydrate, 5 g fat (1 g saturated fat), 40 mg cholesterol, 1,045 mg sodium.

Chicken, Bean, & Tomato Stir-Fry

If you think good taste is hard to measure, consider Chinese long beans. A star of Asian stir-fries, these dark green, pencil-thin legumes average 1½ feet of meaty, crunchy flavor. (Also pictured on the cover.)

6 ounces wide rice noodles or dried egg noodles
12 ounces skinless, boneless chicken breast halves
1 teaspoon Cajun seasoning or other spicy seasoning blend
4 teaspoons cooking oil
2 cloves garlic, minced
1 pound Chinese long beans or whole green beans, cut into 3-inch pieces
¼ cup water
2 medium tomatoes, cut into thin wedges
2 tablespoons raspberry vinegar

Cook rice noodles in boiling, lightly salted water for 3 to 5 minutes or till tender. (Or, cook egg noodles according to package directions.) Drain; keep warm. Meanwhile, rinse chicken; pat dry with paper towels. Cut into thin bite-size strips. Toss chicken with Cajun or other seasoning. Set aside.

Add 2 teaspoons of the oil to a large skillet. Preheat over medium-high heat. Stir-fry garlic in hot oil for 15 seconds. Add beans. Stir-fry for 2 minutes. Add water; reduce heat to low. Cover and simmer for 6 to 8 minutes or till beans are crisp-tender. Remove beans.

Add the remaining oil to skillet. Add chicken. Stir-fry for 2 to 3 minutes or till tender and no longer pink. Return cooked beans to skillet. Add tomatoes and vinegar. Stir all ingredients together to coat. Cook and stir for 1 to 2 minutes more or till heated through. Serve immediately over noodles. Makes 4 servings.

Nutrition information per serving: 361 calories, 25 g protein, 54 g carbohydrate, 5 g fat (1 g saturated fat), 45 mg cholesterol, 334 mg sodium.

Stir-Frying Garlic

To evenly distribute garlic flavor to stir-fry ingredients, season the oil by adding the garlic first. Add the garlic to the hot oil, keeping it moving constantly so it doesn't burn. After about 15 seconds, begin adding the other stir-fry ingredients to the oil.

Turkey-Apricot Stir-Fry

Tangy apricots make this sweet-and-sour entrée pleasantly different from other stir-fries.

12 ounces turkey breast tenderloin
    steaks
½ cup apricot or peach nectar
3 tablespoons soy sauce
2 tablespoons rice vinegar or white
    vinegar
1 tablespoon cornstarch
¼ teaspoon ground red pepper
½ cup dried apricot halves, cut in half
1 tablespoon cooking oil
1 small onion, chopped (⅓ cup)
2 cups fresh pea pods, strings
    removed, or one 6-ounce package
    frozen pea pods, thawed
1 small red or green sweet pepper,
    cut into 1-inch pieces
2 cups hot cooked couscous or rice

Rinse turkey; pat dry with paper towels. Cut into thin bite-size strips. Set aside.

For sauce, in a small bowl stir together apricot or peach nectar, soy sauce, vinegar, cornstarch, and ground red pepper. Stir in apricots. Set aside.

Add cooking oil to a wok or large skillet. Preheat over medium-high heat (add more oil if necessary during cooking). Stir-fry onion in hot oil for 1 minute. Add fresh pea pods (if using) and sweet pepper. Stir-fry for 1 to 2 minutes more or till vegetables are crisp-tender. Remove vegetables from wok.

Add turkey to wok. Stir-fry for 2 to 3 minutes or till tender and no longer pink. Push from center of wok.

Stir sauce; add to center of wok. Cook and stir till thickened and bubbly. Return cooked vegetables to wok. If using, add thawed frozen pea pods. Stir all ingredients together to coat. Cook and stir about 1 minute more or till heated through.

Serve immediately over hot cooked couscous or rice. Makes 4 servings.

Nutrition information per serving: 325 calories, 23 g protein, 46 g carbohydrate, 6 g fat (1 g saturated fat), 37 mg cholesterol, 817 mg sodium.

Pineapple-Orange Ginger Turkey

This easy-to-fix Polynesian-style dish capitalizes on the tangy-sweet flavors of pineapple and orange juice concentrate plus a generous amount of fresh ginger.

1 pound turkey breast tenderloin steaks
2 tablespoons soy sauce
2 tablespoons dry sherry
½ of a 6-ounce can (⅓ cup) frozen orange juice concentrate, thawed
2 tablespoons soy sauce
1 tablespoon water
2 teaspoons cornstarch
½ teaspoon sugar
1 tablespoon cooking oil
2 to 3 teaspoons grated gingerroot
1 medium red or green sweet pepper, cut into bite-size strips
1 8-ounce can pineapple chunks, (juice pack), drained
2 cups hot cooked rice
Orange slices (optional)
Fresh rosemary sprigs (optional)

Rinse turkey; pat dry with paper towels. Cut into thin bite-size strips. In a medium bowl stir together turkey, 2 tablespoons soy sauce, and sherry. Cover and chill for 30 minutes to 1 hour.

For sauce, in a small bowl stir together the orange juice concentrate, 2 tablespoons soy sauce, water, cornstarch, and sugar. Set aside.

Add cooking oil to a wok or large skillet. Preheat over medium-high heat (add more oil if necessary during cooking). Stir-fry gingerroot in hot oil for 15 seconds. Add pepper strips; stir-fry for 1 to 2 minutes or till crisp-tender. Remove pepper strips from wok.

Add half of the turkey mixture to wok. Stir-fry for 2 to 3 minutes or till turkey is tender and no longer pink. Remove turkey from wok. Repeat with the remaining turkey mixture. Return all of the turkey to wok. Push turkey from center of wok.

Stir sauce; add to center of wok. Cook and stir till thickened and bubbly. Return pepper strips to wok. Add pineapple. Stir all ingredients together to coat. Cook and stir about 1 minute more or till mixture is heated through.

Serve immediately with hot rice. If desired, garnish with orange slices and rosemary. Makes 4 servings.

Nutrition information per serving: 352 calories, 25 g protein, 46 g carbohydrate, 6 g fat (1 g saturated fat), 50 mg cholesterol, 1,077 mg sodium.

Shark and Shrimp with Broccoli

Shark, marlin, or swordfish are excellent choices for stir-frying because of their firm texture.

8 ounces fresh or frozen shark, marlin, or swordfish steaks, cut 1 inch thick
8 ounces fresh or frozen, peeled, deveined medium shrimp
2 tablespoons soy sauce
2 tablespoons dry sherry
1 teaspoon grated gingerroot
¾ teaspoon sugar
1 tablespoon cooking oil
1 clove garlic, minced
4 cups broccoli flowerets
1 medium red or green sweet pepper, chopped
2 cups hot cooked Chinese egg noodles or fine noodles

Thaw fish and shrimp, if frozen. Rinse fish and shrimp; pat dry with paper towels. Cut fish into 1-inch cubes. Discard any skin and bones.

In a medium bowl stir together fish, shrimp, soy sauce, sherry, gingerroot, and sugar. Cover and chill for 30 minutes. Drain fish and shrimp, reserving the soy mixture. Set aside.

Add cooking oil to a wok or large skillet. Preheat over medium-high heat (add more oil if necessary during cooking). Stir-fry garlic in hot oil for 15 seconds. Add broccoli; stir-fry for 3 minutes. Add sweet pepper; stir-fry about 1 minute more or till vegetables are crisp-tender. Remove vegetables from wok.

Add half of the fish and shrimp to wok. Stir-fry for 3 to 5 minutes or till fish flakes easily with a fork, being careful not to break up pieces. Remove from wok. Repeat with the remaining fish and shrimp. Return all of the fish and shrimp to wok. Push fish and shrimp from center of wok.

Add soy mixture to center of wok. Cook and stir till bubbly. Return cooked vegetables to wok. Gently stir all ingredients together to coat. Cook and stir for 1 to 2 minutes more or till heated through. Serve immediately over hot noodles. Makes 4 servings.

Nutrition information per serving: 298 calories, 28 g protein, 28 g carbohydrate, 8 g fat (2 g saturated fat), 136 mg cholesterol, 695 mg sodium.

Fish Creole

For a refreshingly light entrée, stir-fry fish with the classic flavors of New Orleans—green pepper, celery, onion, and tomatoes.

1 pound fresh or frozen swordfish,
   sea bass, tuna, or tile fish steaks,
   cut 1 inch thick
1 14½-ounce can tomatoes, cut up
½ teaspoon sugar
½ teaspoon salt
⅛ to ¼ teaspoon ground red pepper
1 tablespoon cooking oil
1 medium onion, chopped
1 stalk celery, thinly sliced
1 medium green sweet pepper, cut
   into 2-inch strips
2 tablespoons snipped parsley
2 cups hot cooked rice

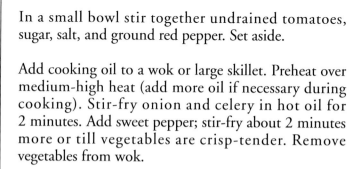

Thaw fish, if frozen. Rinse fish; pat dry with paper towels. Cut into 1-inch cubes. Discard any skin and bones. Set aside.

In a small bowl stir together undrained tomatoes, sugar, salt, and ground red pepper. Set aside.

Add cooking oil to a wok or large skillet. Preheat over medium-high heat (add more oil if necessary during cooking). Stir-fry onion and celery in hot oil for 2 minutes. Add sweet pepper; stir-fry about 2 minutes more or till vegetables are crisp-tender. Remove vegetables from wok.

Add half of the fish to wok. Stir-fry for 3 to 5 minutes or till fish flakes easily with a fork, being careful not to break up pieces. Remove from wok. Repeat with the remaining fish. Remove all of the fish from wok.

Add the tomato mixture to wok. Return the cooked vegetables to wok. Stir all ingredients together to coat. Cook and stir about 3 minutes or till slightly thickened. Add parsley. Gently stir in fish. Cook for 1 to 2 minutes more or till heated through. Serve immediately in bowls over hot rice. Makes 4 servings.

Nutrition information per serving: 311 calories, 26 g protein, 31 g carbohydrate, 9 g fat (2 g saturated fat), 45 mg cholesterol, 569 mg sodium.

Almond Shrimp in Plum Sauce

Plums, cucumber, and onion make this sweet-and-sour dish especially tasty. Toasted almonds lend additional flavor and a bit of crunch!

12	ounces fresh or frozen, peeled, deveined medium shrimp
¼	cup orange juice
¼	cup water
3	tablespoons sugar
3	tablespoons hoisin sauce
2	tablespoons vinegar
4	teaspoons cornstarch
¼	teaspoon pepper
3	tablespoons slivered almonds
1	tablespoon cooking oil
1½	teaspoons grated gingerroot
1	medium onion, chopped
4	medium red plums, pitted and thinly sliced (2 cups)
1	medium cucumber, seeded and chopped (1¼ cups)
2	cups hot cooked rice

Thaw shrimp, if frozen. Rinse shrimp; pat dry with paper towels. Set aside.

For sauce, in a small bowl stir together orange juice, water, sugar, hoisin sauce, vinegar, cornstarch, and pepper. Set aside.

Preheat a wok or large skillet over medium-high heat. Add almonds; stir-fry for 2 to 3 minutes or till golden. Remove almonds from wok. Let wok cool.

Add cooking oil to wok. Preheat over medium-high heat (add more oil if necessary during cooking). Stir-fry gingerroot in hot oil for 15 seconds. Add onion; stir-fry for 3 to 4 minutes or till crisp-tender. Add plums and cucumber; stir-fry for 2 minutes more. Remove plum mixture from wok.

Add shrimp to wok. Stir-fry for 2 to 3 minutes or till shrimp turn pink. Push shrimp from center of wok.

Stir sauce; add to center of wok. Cook and stir till thickened and bubbly. Return plum mixture to wok. Stir all ingredients together to coat. Cook and stir for 1 to 2 minutes more or till heated through. Serve immediately with hot cooked rice. Sprinkle with toasted almonds. Makes 4 servings.

Nutrition information per serving: 345 calories, 19 g protein, 51 g carbohydrate, 8 g fat (1 g saturated fat), 131 mg cholesterol, 926 mg sodium.

Shrimp Piccata

Lemon, garlic, and white wine characterize this exceptionally easy, but oh-so-elegant, entrée. Accompany the meal with crisp-tender stalks of steamed asparagus and garnish with scored lemon slices.

1 pound fresh or frozen, peeled, deveined large shrimp
2 tablespoons all-purpose flour
⅓ cup dry white wine
2 tablespoons lemon juice
1 tablespoon capers, drained
¼ teaspoon salt
⅛ teaspoon pepper
1 tablespoon margarine or butter
2 cloves garlic, minced
2 cups hot cooked brown rice and wild rice
  Lemon slices, halved (optional)

Thaw shrimp, if frozen. Rinse shrimp; pat dry with paper towels. In a medium bowl toss shrimp with flour till coated. Set aside.

For sauce, in a small bowl stir together wine, lemon juice, capers, salt, and pepper. Set aside.

Add the margarine or butter to a wok or large skillet. Preheat over medium-high heat till margarine is melted (add more margarine if necessary during cooking). Stir-fry garlic in margarine for 15 seconds.

Add half of the shrimp to wok. Stir-fry for 2 to 3 minutes or till shrimp turn pink. Remove from wok. Repeat with the remaining shrimp. Remove all of the shrimp from wok.

Add sauce to wok. Cook and stir till sauce is bubbly and reduces slightly. Return shrimp to wok. Cook and stir about 1 minute more or till heated through.

Serve immediately over a mixture of cooked brown rice and wild rice. If desired, garnish with lemon slices. Makes 4 servings.

Nutrition information per serving: 247 calories, 21 g protein, 27 g carbohydrate, 4 g fat (1 g saturated fat), 174 mg cholesterol, 405 mg sodium.

Scallops in Curry Sauce

Because of their larger size, sea scallops work better than bay scallops for stir-frying. Choose scallops that are firm, sweet smelling, and free of excess cloudy liquid.

12	ounces fresh or frozen sea scallops
1	cup water
1	tablespoon cornstarch
2	teaspoons soy sauce
1	teaspoon sugar
1	tablespoon cooking oil
2	teaspoons grated gingerroot
4	cloves garlic, minced
3	stalks celery, thinly bias-sliced
2	medium carrots, thinly bias-sliced
4	ounces fresh mushrooms, quartered (1½ cups)
4	green onions, cut into 1-inch pieces (⅔ cup)
1	teaspoon curry powder
2	cups hot cooked rice
⅓	cup chutney
	Toasted pita wedges (optional)

Thaw scallops, if frozen. Rinse scallops; pat dry with paper towels. Cut any large scallops in half. Set aside.

For sauce, in a small bowl stir together the water, cornstarch, soy sauce, and sugar. Set aside.

Add cooking oil to a wok or large skillet. Preheat over medium-high heat (add more oil if necessary during cooking). Stir-fry the gingerroot and garlic in hot oil for 15 seconds. Add celery and carrots; stir-fry for 2 minutes. Add mushrooms and green onions; stir-fry for 1 minute. Sprinkle curry powder over vegetables. Stir-fry about 1 minute more or till vegetables are crisp-tender. Remove vegetables from wok.

Add scallops to wok. Stir-fry about 2 minutes or till scallops are opaque. Push scallops from center of wok.

Stir sauce; add to center of wok. Cook and stir till thickened and bubbly. Return cooked vegetables to wok. Gently stir all ingredients together to coat. Cook and stir for 1 to 2 minutes more or till heated through.

Serve immediately with hot cooked rice, chutney, and, if desired, pita wedges. Makes 4 servings.

Nutrition information per serving: 290 calories, 15 g protein, 48 g carbohydrate, 5 g fat (1 g saturated fat), 25 mg cholesterol, 359 mg sodium.

Curried Vegetable Stir-Fry

This flavorful vegetable entrée fuses Asian stir-frying with curry and European Brussels sprouts.

2 cups water

1¼ cups quick-cooking pearl barley

1 cup fresh Brussels sprouts, halved, or frozen Brussels sprouts, thawed and halved

1 cup cold water

4 teaspoons cornstarch

1 to 2 teaspoons curry powder

1 teaspoon instant vegetable bouillon granules

  Nonstick spray coating

2 medium red, yellow, and/or green sweet peppers, cut into bite-size strips (1½ cups)

2 tablespoons thinly sliced green onion

1 cup bias-sliced carrots

¼ cup peanuts

Bring 2 cups water to boiling. Stir in barley. Return to boiling; reduce heat. Simmer, covered, for 10 to 12 minutes or till tender. If necessary, drain. Cook Brussels sprouts in a small amount of boiling water for 3 minutes. Drain. For sauce, stir together 1 cup water, cornstarch, curry powder, and bouillon granules.

Spray an unheated wok or large skillet with nonstick coating. Preheat over medium-high heat. Stir-fry the peppers and green onion in hot wok for 1 minute. Add the Brussels sprouts and carrots; stir-fry for 3 minutes. Push from center of wok. Stir sauce; add to center of wok. Cook and stir till thickened and bubbly. Stir all ingredients together to coat. Cook and stir for 2 minutes more. Serve immediately over barley. Sprinkle with peanuts. Makes 4 servings.

Nutrition information per serving: 320 calories, 10 g protein, 59 g carbohydrate, 6 g fat (1 g saturated fat), 0 mg cholesterol, 333 mg sodium.

Mu Shu Vegetable Roll-Ups

Instead of wrapping up our Mu Shu vegetables in the traditional Peking pancakes, we went Mexican and used ready-made flour tortillas. For easier handling, be sure to warm the tortillas before filling.

2 tablespoons water
2 tablespoons soy sauce
½ teaspoon sugar
½ teaspoon cornstarch
8 to 10 8-inch flour tortillas
1 tablespoon cooking oil
1 teaspoon grated gingerroot
2 cloves garlic, minced
2 medium carrots, cut into julienne strips
½ of a small head cabbage, shredded (3 cups)
1 medium zucchini, cut into julienne strips (1¼ cups)
4 cups sliced fresh mushrooms
2 cups fresh bean sprouts
½ of a medium jicama, peeled and cut into julienne strips (1 cup)
8 ounces firm tofu (bean curd), well drained and cut into ¾-inch cubes
8 green onions, sliced (1 cup)
¼ cup hoisin sauce
Cherry tomato flowers (optional)
Green onion brushes (optional)

For sauce, in a small bowl stir together water, soy sauce, sugar, and cornstarch. Set aside.

Wrap tortillas in foil and bake in a 350° oven about 10 minutes or till warm. [Or, just before serving, microwave tortillas, covered, on 100% power (high) about 1 minute or till warm.]

Meanwhile, pour cooking oil into a wok or large skillet. Preheat over medium-high heat (add more oil if necessary during cooking). Stir-fry gingerroot and garlic in hot oil for 15 seconds. Add carrots; stir-fry for 1 minute. Add cabbage and zucchini; stir-fry for 1 minute. Add mushrooms, bean sprouts, and jicama. Stir-fry for 1 to 2 minutes more or till vegetables are crisp-tender. Push vegetables from center of wok.

Stir sauce; add to center of wok. Cook and stir till thickened and bubbly. Add tofu and sliced green onions. Gently stir all ingredients together to coat. Cover and cook about 2 minutes more or till mixture is heated through.

Spread warm tortillas with hoisin sauce. Spoon the vegetable mixture onto each tortilla. Fold over one side of tortilla to cover some of the filling. Then fold the two adjacent sides of tortilla over filling. Secure with toothpicks, if necessary. Serve immediately. If desired, garnish with tomato flowers and green onion brushes. Makes 4 or 5 servings.

Nutrition information per serving: 399 calories, 20 g protein, 57 g carbohydrate, 12 g fat (2 g saturated fat), 0 mg cholesterol, 1,811 mg sodium.

Mandarin Tofu Stir-Fry

Tofu takes on the flavors you mix with it. In this case, a sweet-and-sour sauce does the trick.

½ cup sweet-and-sour sauce
⅛ teaspoon ground red pepper
1 tablespoon cooking oil
6 green onions, bias-sliced into
    1-inch pieces (1 cup)
½ of a medium red or green sweet
    pepper, cut into strips
2 cups fresh pea pods, strings
    removed, or one 6-ounce package
    frozen pea pods, thawed
1 pound firm tofu (bean curd), well
    drained and cut into ¾-inch cubes
1 11-ounce can mandarin orange
    sections, drained, or 3 medium
    oranges, peeled and sectioned
2 cups hot cooked rice
2 tablespoons unsalted dry roasted
    peanuts

For sauce, in a small bowl stir together sweet-and-sour sauce and ground red pepper. Set aside.

Add cooking oil to a wok or large skillet. Preheat over medium-high heat (add more oil if necessary during cooking). Stir-fry green onions and sweet pepper in hot oil for 1 minute. If using, add fresh pea pods; stir-fry for 1 to 2 minutes more or till vegetables are crisp-tender. Push vegetables from center of wok.

Add sauce to center of wok. Cook and stir till bubbly. Add tofu, orange sections, and, if using, thawed frozen pea pods. Gently stir all ingredients together to coat. Cover and cook for 1 to 2 minutes more or till heated through. Serve immediately with hot cooked rice. Sprinkle with peanuts. Makes 4 servings.

Nutrition information per serving: 360 calories, 15 g protein, 53 g carbohydrate, 12 g fat (2 g saturated fat), 0 mg cholesterol, 117 mg sodium.

Sesame Vegetables

In this Chinese-style dish, toasted sesame oil and sesame seed give the vegetables an added flavor boost.

2 tablespoons soy sauce
½ teaspoon sugar
½ teaspoon toasted sesame oil
1 tablespoon cooking oil
1 teaspoon grated gingerroot
2 cloves garlic, minced
2 cups broccoli flowerets
12 ounces asparagus, trimmed and
   bias-sliced into 1-inch pieces
   (2 cups)
2 small yellow summer squash, halved
   lengthwise and sliced ¼ inch
   thick (2 cups)
1½ cups sliced fresh mushrooms
1 tablespoon sesame seed
2 green onions, sliced (¼ cup)

For sauce, stir together soy sauce, sugar, and sesame oil. Set aside. Add cooking oil to a wok or 12-inch skillet. Preheat over medium-high heat (add more oil if necessary during cooking). Stir-fry the gingerroot and garlic in hot oil for 15 seconds. Add broccoli and asparagus; stir-fry about 4 minutes or till vegetables are crisp-tender. Remove broccoli mixture from wok.

Add squash, mushrooms, and sesame seed to wok. Stir-fry for 2 to 3 minutes or till crisp-tender. Return broccoli mixture to wok. Stir in onions and sauce. Cook and stir for 1 to 2 minutes or till heated through. Serve immediately. Makes 4 to 6 side-dish servings.

Nutrition information per serving: 117 calories, 6 g protein, 14 g carbohydrate, 6 g fat (1 g saturated fat), 0 mg cholesterol, 540 mg sodium.

Butter-Glazed Summer Vegetables

This simple dish, with its sprinkling of fragrant herbs, enhances the natural goodness of summer vegetables.

1 tablespoon cooking oil
2 small zucchini, thinly bias-sliced
   (2 cups)
2 small yellow summer squash, thinly
   bias-sliced (2 cups)
2 cups broccoli flowerets
2 teaspoons snipped fresh basil
2 teaspoons snipped fresh oregano
¼ teaspoon salt
⅛ teaspoon pepper
1 medium tomato, chopped
1 tablespoon butter or margarine

Add cooking oil to a wok or large skillet. Preheat over medium-high heat (add more oil if necessary during cooking). Stir-fry zucchini and yellow squash in hot oil for 3 to 4 minutes or till crisp-tender. Remove.

Add broccoli, basil, oregano, salt, and pepper to wok. Stir-fry for 2 to 3 minutes or till crisp-tender. Return cooked squash to wok. Stir in tomato and butter or margarine. Cook and stir just till butter is melted. Serve immediately. Makes 4 to 6 side-dish servings.

Nutrition information per serving: 97 calories, 3 g protein, 8 g carbohydrate, 7 g fat (2 g saturated fat), 8 mg cholesterol, 187 mg sodium.

INDEX